Greenhouse Effect

James F. Frayne

MONTANA PUBLISHERS

All characters appearing in this work are fictitious. Any resemblance to real persons, living or dead, is purely coincidental.

First Printing: 2018

ISBN: 978-0-244-15851-4

Montana Publishers

Ordering information:
Special discounts are available on quantity purchases by corporations, associations, educators, and others. For details, contact the publisher at the e-mail address detailed below.

U.S. trade bookstores and wholesalers:

Please contact publishers at: e-mail
TGTG2014@hotmail.com

By the same author:

Tall Grows the Grass (Novel)
First Son of Khui (Novel)

Easy as you Go! A Mathematical Companion
(Volume 1: A – L)
Easy as you Go! A Mathematical Companion
(Volume 2: M- Z)
A-Star Question Bank
(Mathematics with or without solutions)
Mathematics & Statistics for Biology, Psychology &
Chemistry

Hell Bank Notes (A Pictorial Catalogue)
Romancing the Wood
(History behind the American Wooden Nickel)
The Indian Hundi
(Favourite negotiable instrument in days gone by)
Hidden Stories behind Paper Money around the World

Selected Biology Advance Level Topics (Volume 1: A – J)
Selected Biology Advance Level Topics (Volume 2: K – Z)

Advanced Level Biology

Applications of Genetics
Atoms and Fundamental Particles

Mathematics by Stages (Angles to Vectors)
Mathematics by Stages (Circles and Curves)
Mathematics by Stages
(Trigonometrical Identities and the Calculus)

Jenny Two-tails and her Friends (Book for Young Children)

For more details please visit author's website at:
jamesfrayne.co.uk

5

Greenhouse Effect

Contents

Preface

While other planets in Earth's solar system are either scorching hot or
bitterly cold, Earth's surface has relatively mild, stable temperatures.
Earth enjoys these temperatures because of its atmosphere, which is
the thin layer of gases that cloak and protect the planet. In fact, if there
was no water vapour, the average temperature of Earth would be about
19^0C cooler overall.

It is generally agreed now that humans have changed Earth's
atmosphere in dramatic ways over the past two centuries, resulting in
global warming. To understand global warming though, it's first
necessary to become familiar with the greenhouse effect.

There's a delicate balancing act occurring every day all across the
Earth, involving the radiation the planet receives from space and the
radiation that's reflected back out to space. Earth is constantly
bombarded with enormous amounts of radiation, primarily from the
sun. This solar radiation strikes the Earth's atmosphere in the form of
visible light, plus ultraviolet (UV), infrared (IR) and other types of
radiation that are invisible to the human eye.

UV radiation has a shorter wavelength and a higher energy level than
visible light, while IR radiation has a longer wavelength and a weaker
energy level. It is estimated that about 30 percent of the radiation
striking Earth's atmosphere is immediately reflected back out to space
by clouds, ice, snow, sand and other reflective surfaces. The remaining
70 percent of incoming solar radiation is absorbed by the oceans, the
land and the atmosphere. As they heat up, the oceans, land and
atmosphere release heat in the form of IR thermal radiation, which
passes out of the atmosphere and into space.

It is this equilibrium of incoming and outgoing radiation that makes the
Earth habitable, with an average temperature of about 15^0C.

Notes:

11

Without this atmospheric equilibrium, Earth would be as cold and lifeless as its moon, or as blazing hot as Venus. The moon, which has almost no atmosphere, is about minus 153^0C) on its dark side. Venus, on the other hand, has a very dense atmosphere that traps solar radiation; the average temperature on Venus is about 462^0C.

The Greenhouse Effect

The exchange of incoming and outgoing radiation that warms the Earth is often referred to as the greenhouse effect because a greenhouse works in much the same way.

Carbon dioxide (CO_2) and other greenhouse gases act like a blanket, absorbing IR radiation and preventing it from escaping into outer space. The net effect is the gradual heating of Earth's atmosphere and surface, a process known as global warming. These greenhouse gases include water vapour, CO_2, methane, nitrous oxide (N_2O), carbon monoxide (CO) and other gases.

Since the dawn of the Industrial Revolution in the early 1800s, the burning of fossil fuels like coal, oil and gasoline have greatly increased the concentration of greenhouse gases in the atmosphere, especially CO_2. Deforestation is the second largest anthropogenic source of carbon dioxide to the atmosphere ranging between 6 percent and 17 percent.

Atmospheric CO_2 levels have increased by more than 40 percent since the beginning of the Industrial Revolution, from about 280 parts per million (ppm) in the 1800s to 400 ppm today. The last time Earth's atmospheric levels of CO_2 reached 400 ppm was during the Pliocene Epoch, between 5 million and 3 million years ago.

Notes:

The greenhouse effect, combined with increasing levels of greenhouse gases and the resulting global warming, is expected to have profound implications, according to the near-universal consensus of scientists.

If global warming continues unchecked, it will cause significant climate change, a rise in sea levels, increasing ocean acidification, extreme weather events and other severe natural and societal impacts.

Yet we must never forget that CO_2 gas is not the only greenhouse gas. Along with CO_2, and discounting water vapour, we have, as mentioned above, methane, nitrous oxide and carbon monoxide as well as other less consequential gases.

Atmospheric lifetime and GWP relative to CO_2 at different time horizons for various greenhouse gases

Gas name	Chemical formula	Lifetime (years)	Global warming potential (GWP) for given time horizon		
			20-yr	100-yr	500-yr
Carbon dioxide	CO_2	Variable	1	1	1
Methane	CH_4	12	72	25	7.6
Nitrous oxide	N_2O	114	289	298	153
CFC-12	CCl_2F_2	100	11 000	10 900	5 200
HCFC-22	$CHClF_2$	12	5 160	1 810	549
Tetrafluoromethane	CF_4	50 000	5 210	7 390	11 200
Hexafluoroethane	C_2F_6	10 000	8 630	12 200	18 200
Sulphur hexafluoride	SF_6	3 200	16 300	22 800	32 600
Nitrogen trifluoride	NF_3	740	12 300	17 200	20 700

Notes:

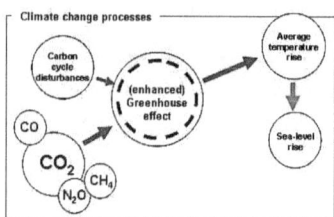

Climate Change Processes

Water vapour which is considered a necessary greenhouse gas and, without it, life on Earth would be very different. For this reason, it is not usually considered when looking at the effects of global warming. Earth therefore has a natural greenhouse effect, but this is being put out of balance by the various anthropomorphic effects, notably from carbon dioxide, methane, nitrous oxide, and to a lesser extent, carbon monoxide and other gasses.

Notes:

14

Greenhouse gases are components of the atmosphere that contribute to the greenhouse effect.

Without the greenhouse effect the Earth would be uninhabitable; in its absence, the mean temperature of the earth would be about -19^0C rather than the present mean temperature of about 15^0C.

Greenhouse gases come from natural sources and human activity. This causes the "Greenhouse Effect".

Carbon Dioxide

Carbon Dioxide (CO_2) is a colourless, odourless non-flammable gas and is the most prominent greenhouse gas in Earth's atmosphere.

It is recycled through the atmosphere by the process **photosynthesis**, which makes human life possible. Carbon Dioxide is emitted into the air as humans exhale, burn fossil fuels for energy, and deforest the planet. Every year humans add over 30 billion tons of carbon dioxide in the atmosphere by these processes, and it is up thirty percent since 1750.

Methane

Methane is a colourless, odourless, flammable gas. It is formed when plants decay and where there is very little air. It is often called swamp gas because it is abundant around water and swamps.

Bacteria that breakdown organic matter in wetlands and bacteria that are found in cows, sheep, goats, buffalo, termites, and camels produce methane naturally.

Notes:

15

Since 1750, methane has doubled, and could double again by 2050.

Each year we add 350-500 million tons of methane to the air by raising livestock, coal mining, drilling for oil and natural gas, rice cultivation, and garbage landfills.

It stays in the atmosphere for only 12 years, but traps 20 times more heat than carbon dioxide.

Nitrous Oxide

Nitrous oxide is another colourless greenhouse gas, however, it has a sweet odour. This gas is released naturally from oceans and by bacteria in soils.

Nitrous oxide gas has risen by more than 15% since 1750. Each year we add 7-13 million tons into the atmosphere by using nitrogen based fertilizers, disposing of human and animal waste in sewage treatment plants, automobile exhaust, and other sources not yet identified.

It is important to reduce emissions because the nitrous oxide we release today will still be trapped in the atmosphere 100 years from now.

Notes:

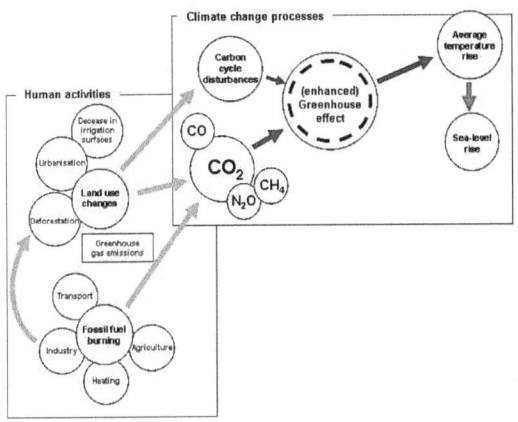

Human Activities

Global warming is the result of increasing atmospheric carbon dioxide concentrations.

This is caused primarily by the combustion of fossil energy sources such as petroleum, coal, and natural gas, and to an unknown extent by destruction of forests, increased methane, volcanic activity, and aluminium and cement production.

Notes:

17

Such massive alteration of the global carbon cycle has only been possible because of the availability and deployment of advanced technologies.

These range in application from fossil fuel exploration, extraction, distribution, refining, and combustion in power plants and automobile engines.

Human impact on the nitrogen cycle is diverse. Agricultural and industrial nitrogen inputs to the environment currently exceed inputs from natural nitrogen fixation.

As a consequence of anthropogenic inputs, the global nitrogen cycle has been significantly altered over the past century.

Global atmospheric nitrous oxide (N_2O) mole fractions have increased from a pre-industrial value of ~270 nmol/mol to ~319 nmol/mol in 2005.

Human activities account for over one-third of N_2O emissions, most of which are due to the agricultural sector.

Notes:

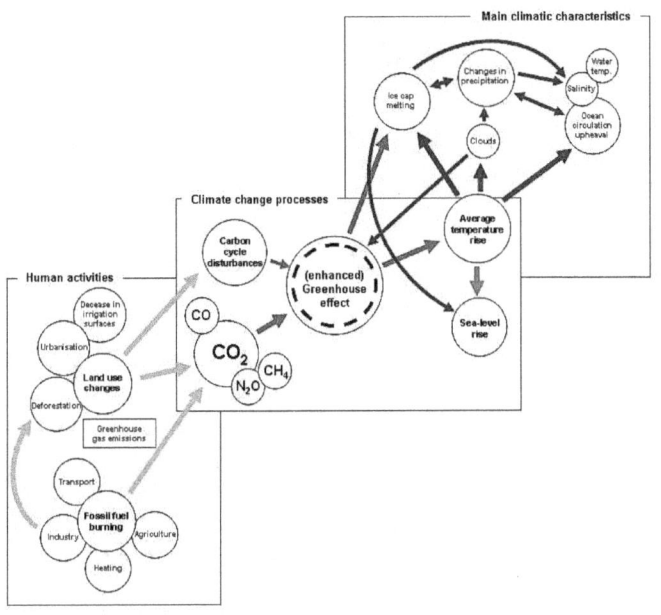

Main Climatic Characteristics

Potential negative environmental impacts caused by increasing atmospheric carbon dioxide concentrations are rising global air temperatures. Altered hydrogeological cycles are causing more frequent and severe droughts, storms, and floods, as well as sea level rise and ecosystem disruption.

Notes:

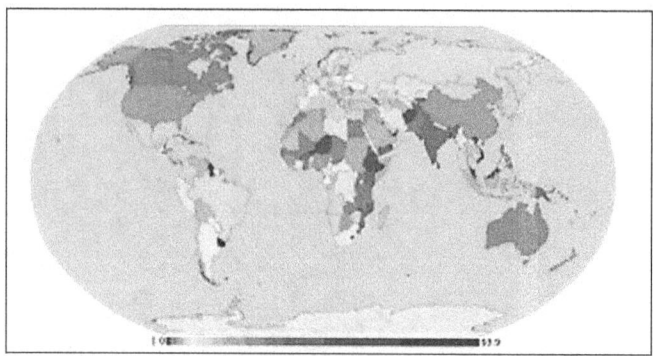

Per capita greenhouse gas emissions by country for the year 2000
including land-use change

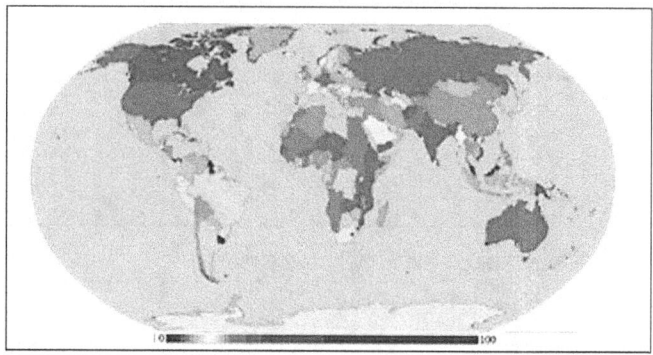

Per capita responsibility for current anthropogenic atmospheric CO_2

Notes:

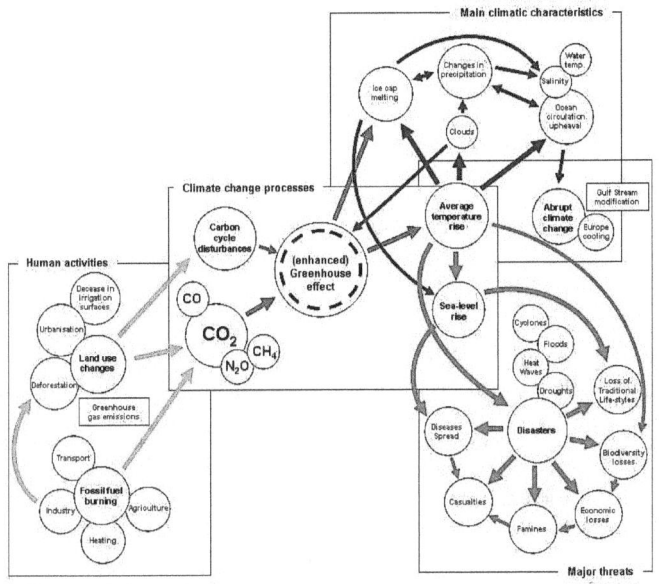

Major Threats

Grasslands contribute to soil organic matter, stored mainly in their extensive fibrous root mats.

Due in part to the climatic conditions of these regions (eg: cooler temperatures and semi-arid to arid conditions), these soils can accumulate significant quantities of organic matter.

Notes:

This can vary based on rainfall, the length of the winter season, and the frequency of naturally occurring lightning-induced grass-fires. While these fires release carbon dioxide, they improve the quality of the grasslands overall, in turn increasing the amount of carbon retained in the humic material. They also deposit carbon directly to the soil in the form of char that does not significantly degrade back to carbon dioxide.

Forest fires release absorbed carbon back into the atmosphere, as does deforestation due to rapidly increased oxidation of soil organic matter.

Organic matter in peat bogs undergoes slow anaerobic decomposition below the surface. This process is slow enough that in many cases the bog grows rapidly and fixes more carbon from the atmosphere than is released. Over time, the peat grows deeper. Peat bogs take up approximately one-quarter of the carbon stored in land plants and soils.

Under some conditions, forests and peat bogs may become sources of CO_2, such as when a forest is flooded. Unless the forests and peat are harvested before flooding, the rotting vegetation is a source of CO_2 and methane comparable in magnitude to the amount of carbon released by a fossil-fuel powered plant of equivalent power.

Notes:

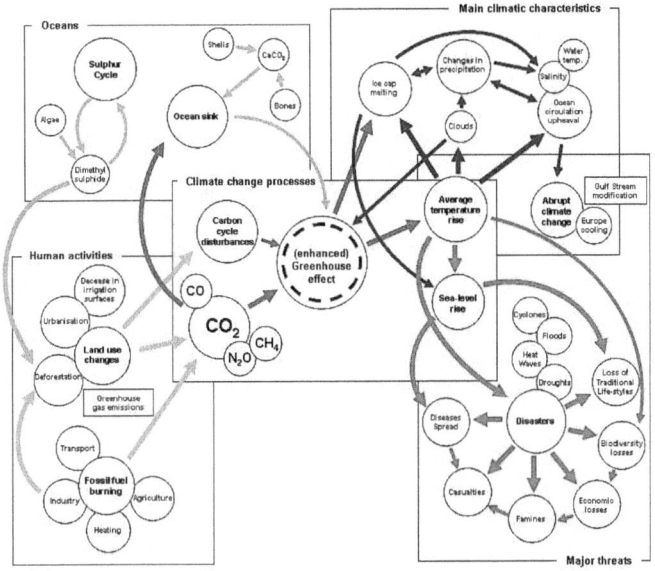

Oceans

A **carbon sink** is a natural or artificial reservoir that accumulates and stores some **carbon-containing chemical compound** for an indefinite period.

The process by which carbon sinks remove carbon dioxide (CO_2) from the atmosphere is known as **carbon sequestration**.

Notes:

23

Kyoto Protocol

Because growing vegetation takes in carbon dioxide, the Kyoto Protocol allows countries with large areas of growing forests to issue Removal Units to recognize the sequestration of carbon.

The additional units make it easier for them to achieve their target emission levels. It is estimated that forests absorb between 10 and 20 tons of carbon dioxide per hectare each year, through photosynthetic conversion into starch, cellulose, lignin, and wooden biomass.

While this has been well documented for temperate forests and plantations, the fauna of the tropical forests place some limitations for such global estimates.

Storage in terrestrial environments

Soils represent a short to long-term carbon storage medium, and contain more carbon than all terrestrial vegetation and the atmosphere combined. Plant litter and other biomass accumulates as organic matter in soils, and is degraded by chemical weathering and biological degradation.

More recalcitrant organic carbon polymers such as cellulose, hemi-cellulose, lignin, aliphatic compounds, waxes and terpenoids are collectively retained as humus.

Areas where shifting cultivation or slash and burn agriculture are practiced are generally only fertile for 2–3 years before they are abandoned. These tropical jungles are similar to coral reefs in that they are highly efficient at conserving and circulating necessary nutrients.

Notes:

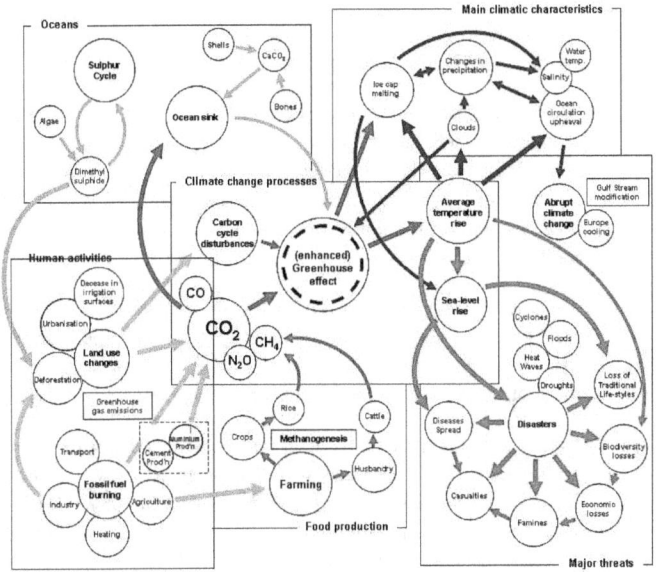

Food Production

Methane emission from **ruminant livestock** is currently estimated to be around 100 million tonnes of methane each year and, after rice agriculture, represents the biggest man-made methane source.

The loss of methane from ruminant livestock is a problem not only in the respect of greenhouse gas emissions, but also to farmers in that food converted into and released as methane is food not being converted into meat and/or milk.

Notes:

25

Methane is produced in the guts of ruminant livestock as a result of methanogenic microorganisms (belonging to the Archaea).

The composition of the animal feed is a crucial factor in controlling the amounts of methane produced, but a sheep can produce about 30 litres of methane each day and a dairy cow up to about 200. At between 50 and 100 million tonnes of methane a year, rice agriculture is a big source of atmospheric methane, possibly the biggest of man-made methane sources.

The warm, waterlogged soil of rice paddies provides ideal conditions for methanogenesis, and though some of the methane produced is usually oxidized by methanotrophs in the shallow overlying water, the vast majority is released into the atmosphere.

Rice is grown very widely and rates of methane emission may vary greatly between different areas. Differences in average temperature, water depth and the length of time that the rice paddy soil is waterlogged can all result in big regional variations. However, methane emission from worldwide rice agriculture has been well studied in recent years and fairly reliable estimates of global emissions now exist.

Agricultural waste can represent a significant source of methane. The anaerobic decomposition of livestock and poultry manure, common to manure heaps and slurry tanks, leads to large amounts of methane production due to its large organic carbon content. Similarly, the processing of industrial and domestic waste water and sewage can also produce significant amounts of methane. In total, such waste accounts for between 14 and 25 million tonnes of methane emission per year globally.

Notes:

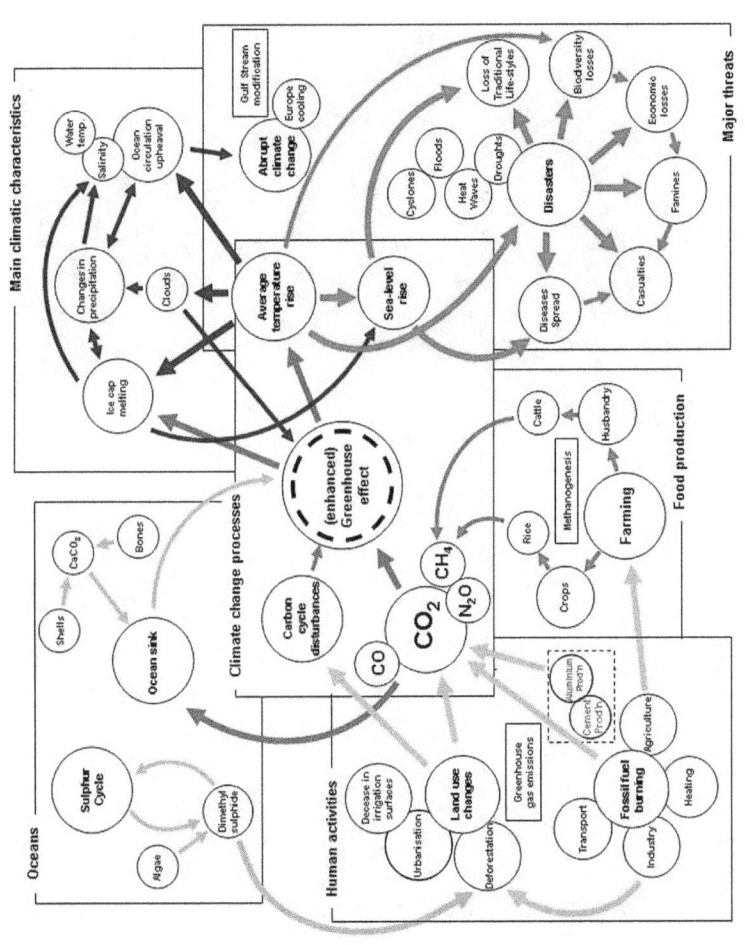

27

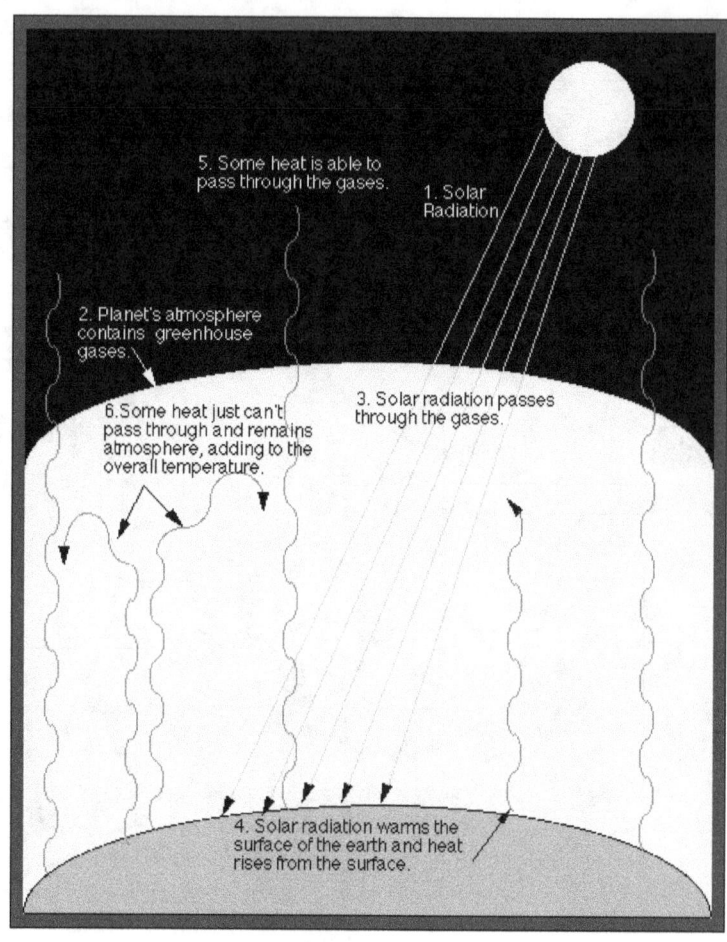

Global Warming
ref: Nick Hopwood and Jordan Cohen

Global Warming is the heating of the Earth due to the presence of greenhouse gases. It is named this way because of a similar effect produced by the glass panes of a greenhouse.

Shorter-wavelength solar radiation from the sun passes through Earth's atmosphere, and then is absorbed by the surface of the Earth, causing it to warm.

Part of the absorbed energy is then reradiated back to the atmosphere as long wave infrared radiation. Little of this long wave radiation escapes back into space; the radiation cannot pass through the greenhouse gases in the atmosphere.

The greenhouse gases selectively transmit the infrared waves, trapping some and allowing some to pass through into space. The greenhouse gases absorb these waves and reemits the waves downward, causing the lower atmosphere to warm.
ref: www.eb.com:180

Greenhouse Gases

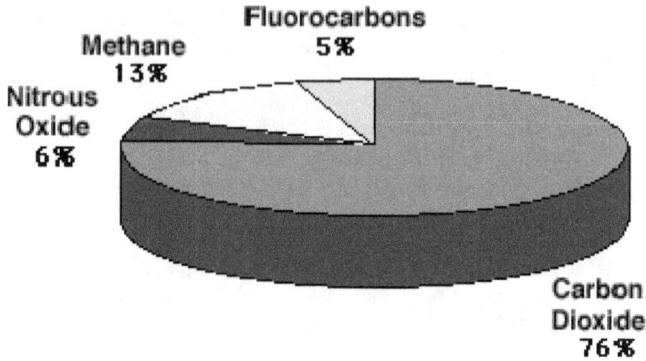

The distribution of Greenhouse Gases in Earth's atmosphere. Carbon Dioxide is clearly the majority.
www.abcnews.com/sections/us/global106.html

Carbon Dioxide

Carbon Dioxide (CO_2) is a colourless, odourless non-flammable gas and is the most prominent Greenhouse gas in Earth's atmosphere.

It is recycled through the atmosphere by the process photosynthesis, which makes human life possible. Photosynthesis is the process of green plants and other organisms transforming light energy into chemical energy. Light Energy is trapped and used to convert carbon dioxide, water, and other minerals into oxygen and energy rich organic compounds.
ref: Encyclopaedia Britannica Volume 25

Carbon Dioxide is emitted into the air as humans exhale, burn fossil fuels for energy, and de-forest the planet. Every year humans add over 30 billion tons of carbon dioxide in the atmosphere by these processes, and it is up thirty percent since 1750.
ref: www.envirolink.org/orgs/edf/sitemap.

An isolated test at Mauna Loa in Hawaii revealed more than a 12% (316 ppm in 1959 to 360 ppm in 1996) increase in mean annual concentration of carbon dioxide. Mauna Loa, located in Hawaii, is the world's largest volcano at 40,000 cubic km and 4,170 meters above sea level.
ref: Encyclopaedia Britannica Volume 27

Ice core samples have also shown a dramatic increase in carbon dioxide levels. Drilling deep into glaciers and polar ice caps and taking out samples of ice, then melting the ice and capturing the gas has shown an increase in carbon dioxide concentrations over the past 100 years. Ice core samples are essentially "drilling through time", because the deeper the ice is, the older the ice is.

In 1996, carbon dioxide world emissions increased by 2.8%. The U.S. reported a 3.3% increase in CO_2 concentrations. The U.S. continues to emit more than any other country in the world, accounting for 25% of all emissions.
ref: http://infoweb.magi.com/~dwalsh/wfsesr

Fossil Fuels were created chiefly by the decay of plants from millions of years ago. We use coal, oil and natural gas to generate electricity, heat our homes, power our factories and run our cars. These fossil fuels contain carbon, and when they are burned, they combine with oxygen, forming carbon dioxide. The two atoms of oxygen add to the total weight.

The World Energy Council reported that global carbon dioxide emissions from burning fossil fuels rose 12% between 1990 and 1995.
ref: www.eb.com:180

The increase from developing countries was three times that from developed countries. Middle East carbon dioxide emissions from burning of fossil fuels increased 35%, Africa increased 12%, and Eastern Europe increased rates by 75% from 1990-1995.

Deforestation is another main producer of carbon dioxide. The causes of deforestation are logging for lumber, pulpwood, and fuel wood.

Also contributing to deforestation is the clearing new land for farming and pastures used for animals such as cows.

Forests and wooded areas are natural carbon sinks. This means that as trees absorb carbon dioxide, and release oxygen, carbon is being put into trees. This process occurs naturally by photosynthesis, which occurs less and less as we cut and burn down trees.

As the abundance of trees declines, less carbon dioxide can be recycled. As we burn them down, carbon is released into the air and the carbon bonds with oxygen to form carbon dioxide, adding to the greenhouse effect. About 860 acres is destroyed every 15 minutes in the tropics.

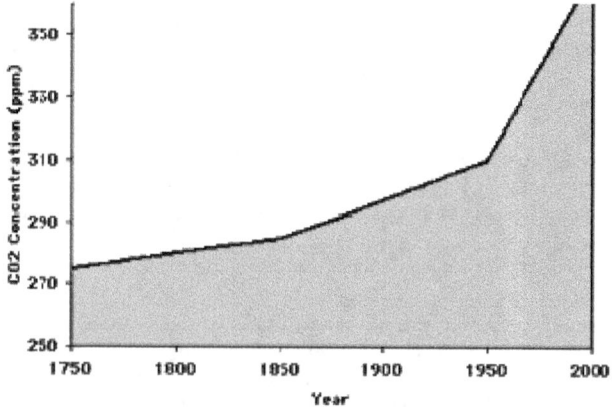

The increase of carbon dioxide in the air over the past few centuries

32

Methane

Methane is a colourless, odourless, flammable gas. It is formed when plants decay and where there is very little air. It is often called *swamp gas* because it is abundant around water and swamps.

Bacteria that breakdown organic matter in wetlands and bacteria that are found in cows, sheep, goats, buffalo, termites, and camels produce methane naturally. Since 1750, methane has doubled, and could double again by 2050. Each year we add 350-500 million tons of methane to the air by raising livestock, coal mining, drilling for oil and natural gas, rice cultivation, and garbage sitting in landfills.
ref: www.envirolink.org/orgs/edf/sitemap

It stays in the atmosphere for only 10 years, but traps 20 times more heat than carbon dioxide.

Rice cultivation has developed into a large business; farmland has doubled in the past 45 years. It feeds one third of the World's population. It grows mostly in flooded fields, where bacteria in waterlogged soil release methane.
ref: www.envirolink.org/orgs/edf/sitemap

Livestock such as cows, sheep, goats, camels, buffaloes, and termites release methane as well. Bacteria in the gut of the animal break down food and convert some of it to methane. When these animals belch, methane is released. In one day, a cow can emit half a pound of methane into the air. Imagine 1.3 billion cattle, every one burping methane several times per minute!

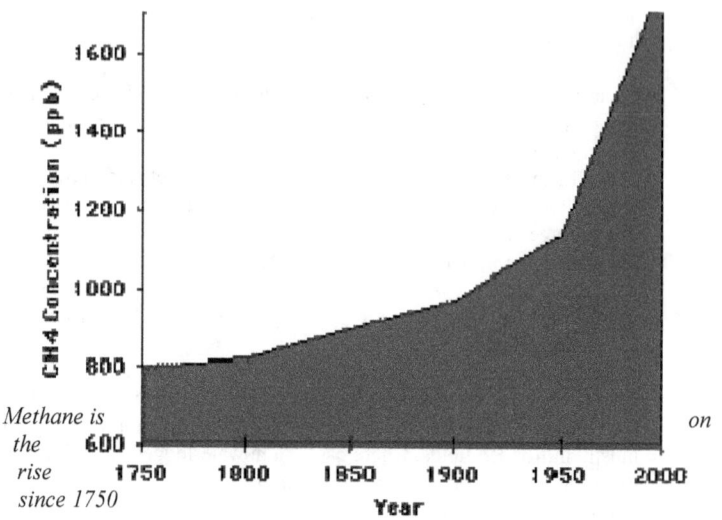

Methane is the rise since 1750 on

www.envirolink.org/orgs/edf/sitemap

34

Nitrous Oxide

Nitrous oxide is another colourless greenhouse gas; however, it has a sweet odour. It is primarily used as an anaesthetic because it deadens pain and for this characteristic is called laughing gas.

This gas is released naturally from oceans and by bacteria in soils. Nitrous oxide gas has risen by more than 15% since 1750. Each year we add 7-13 million tons into the atmosphere by using nitrogen based fertilizers, disposing of human and animal waste in sewage treatment plants, automobile exhaust, and other sources not yet identified.

It is important to reduce emissions because the nitrous oxide we release today will still be trapped in the atmosphere 100 years from now.
ref: World Book Volume 13

Nitrogen based fertilizer use has doubled in the past 15 years. These fertilizers provide nutrients for crops; however, when they breakdown in the soil, nitrous oxide is released into the atmosphere.

In automobiles, nitrous oxide is released at a much lower rate than carbon dioxide, because there is more carbon in petrol than nitrogen.

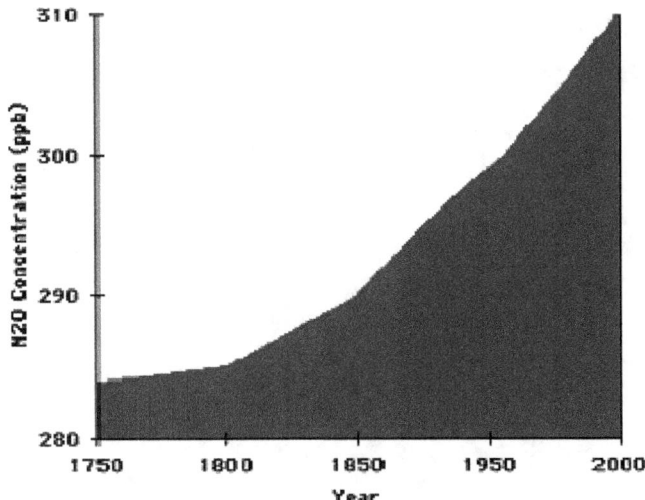

Nitrous Oxide has been on the rise since 1750
www.envirolink.org/orgs/edf/sitmap

35

Fluorocarbons

Fluorocarbons are a general term for any group of synthetic organic compounds that contain fluorine and carbon.

Many of these compounds, such as **chlorofluorocarbons** (CFCs), can be easily converted from gas to liquid or liquid to gas. Because of these properties, CFCs could be used in aerosol cans, refrigerators, and air conditioners. Studies in the 1970s showed that when CFCs are emitted into the atmosphere, they break down molecules in the Earth's ozone layer. Since then, the use of CFCs has significantly decreased and they are banned from production in many countries of the world.

The substitutes for CFCs are **hydrofluorocarbons** (HFCs).

HFCs do not harm or breakdown the ozone molecule, but they do trap heat in the atmosphere, making it a greenhouse gas, and thus aggravating the effect of global warming.

Global Warming is Here!

Naturally, if there are more greenhouse gases in the atmosphere, this greenhouse effect will be more significant and raise the temperature of Earth more than if humans did not emit as much greenhouse gases.

There is no doubt that both land and ocean surface temperatures have gone up significantly in the last 100 years or so, and there is no credible hypothesis for this, other than the net effect of greenhouse gases. The planet is heating up and the evidence suggests that human activities are having a significant impact,
ref: www.abcnew.com/sections/us/global106

The balance of evidence suggests a discernible human influence on global climate which will have severe impacts on human health, natural ecosystems, agriculture, and coastal communities.
ref: www.toowarm.org./factsheets/basfact.html

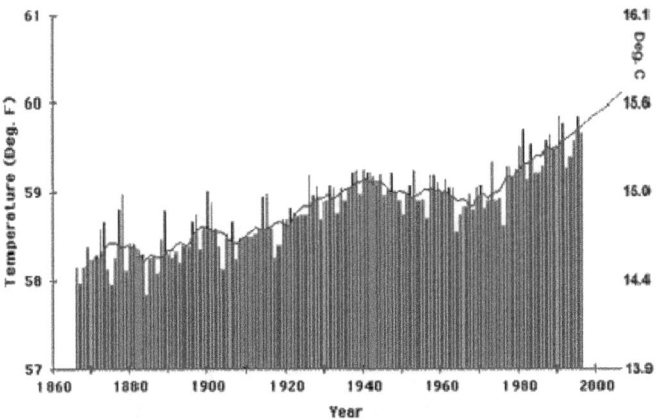

Average yearly temperature rise: 1860-1998
www.evirolink.org/orgs/edf/sitemp

37

Effects of Global Warming on Environment

There are many environmental problems coming from the increase concentration of greenhouse gases in Earth's atmosphere.

Several signs indicate that we've begun changing Earth's climate: increased water vapour in the atmosphere, glaciers and polar ice caps appear to be melting, floods and droughts are becoming more severe, and sea levels have risen, on average, between 4 and 10 inches since 1990.
ref: www.abc.com/sections/us/global106.html

These rises in sea level can increase the salinity of freshwater throughout the world, and cause coastal lands to be washed under the ocean. Warmer water and increased humidity may encourage tropical cyclones, and changing wave patterns could produce more tidal waves and strong beach erosion on the coasts.

Effects of Global Warming on Society

Carbon dioxide is an essential nutrient for the production of food, and food is one of the most important things in our lives. As the temperature rises, more farmland will be open towards the Earth's poles and the length of the growing season will also lengthen.
ref: www.comnett.net/~wit/food

However, this positive effect is outweighed by the increase in the overall amounts of greenhouse gases in the atmosphere. This could lead to considerable health concerns.

As more farmland is made available, insects and other pests will also migrate towards poles. These insects and pests could migrate up to 550 km. Some insects carry diseases such as malaria and dengue fever. Thus, an increase in these particular insects and pests closer to the poles would inevitably result in an increase in these diseases. This could lead to 50 to 80 million additional cases of Malaria annually, a 10-15% increase.

The most obvious health effect is directly from the heat itself. With an increase in heat waves, there will be more people who will suffer from heatstroke, heart attacks and other ailments aggravated by the heat.
ref: www.epa.gov/oppeoee

Hot conditions could also cause smoke particles and noxious gases to linger in the air and accelerate chemical reactions that generate other pollutants. and there is no credible hypothesis for this, other than the net effect of greenhouse gases. This leads to an increase in risk of respiratory diseases like bronchitis and asthma.
ref: www.envirolink.org/orgs/edf/sitemap

Global warming causes the oceans to warm and expand, inducing a rise in sea level. Eventually, the rising waters could take away land inhabited by people, forcing them to move.

Bangladesh cannot afford to build barriers to hold back the sea, so people would have to move inland, increasing the population density and leading to an increase in hunger and disease.
ref: www.envirolink.org/orgs/edf/sitemap

The Maldive Islands in the Indian Ocean have the same problem. They are a nation of 1190 islands with an average height of about 1.5 meters above sea level. If the sea level rises, more than 200,000 people will have to abandon their homes.
ref: www.envirolink.org/orgs/edf/sitmap

Warming of the oceans could also promote toxic algae which can lead to cholera.

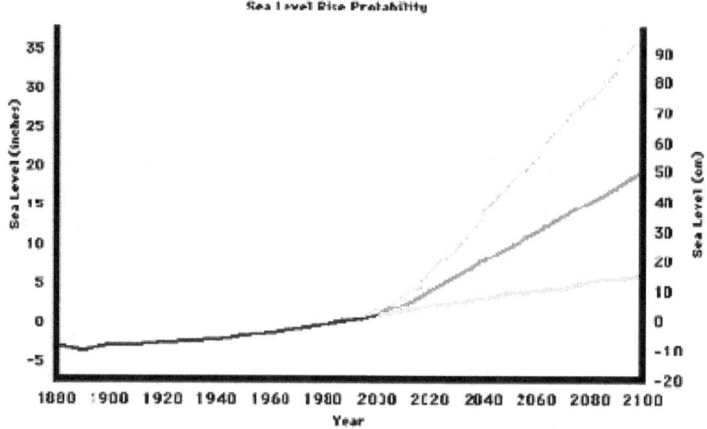

History of sea level and extrapolating possible increases in sea level over the next century
The high line is a high estimate of sea level extrapolated. The middle line a central estimate, and the low bottom is a low projection.
www.envirolink.org/orgs/edf/sitemap.html

Present Ways of Producing Energy

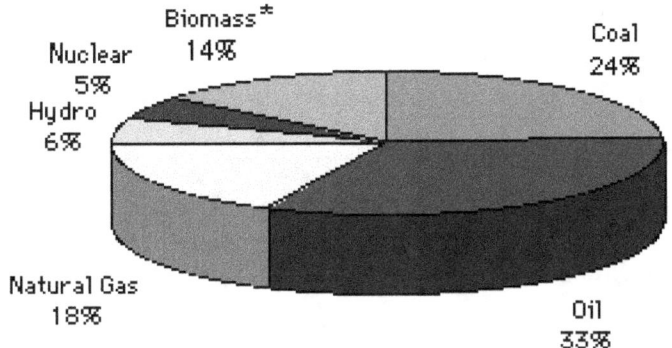

Nuclear 5%

Biomass* 14%

Coal 24%

Hydro 6%

Natural Gas 18%

Oil 33%

Breakdown of how the world produces its energy
www.envirolink.org/orgs/edf/sitemap

Fossil fuels, chiefly coal, oil and natural gas, now supply most of the world's energy.

Only a small amount comes from renewable sources, which do not release gases that trap heat in the atmosphere. If we could get more of our energy from renewable sources, we could reduce the amount of fossil fuels we burn.

By the year 2050, renewable sources could provide forty percent of the energy needed in the world.

Use of renewable energy can help both to slow global warming and to reduce air pollution.

These fossil fuels, coal, oil, and natural gas also emit greenhouse gases when burned. Coal emits high amounts of greenhouse gases, and the world may be supplied with enough of it to last over 100 years. Oil emits high amounts of greenhouse gases and also other types of air pollution harmful to the environment. The world's oil supply is also estimated to last over 100 years. Natural Gas is the lowest of all fossil fuels in greenhouse gas emissions; supplies are projected to last over 100 years.
ref: www.doc.mmu.ac.uk/aric/gcc/cell.html#pos6

1996 Processes Carbon Dioxide was Produced

Country (region)	OIL	Natural Gas	Coal
World	44.7%	18.4%	36.9%
Canada	51.8%	30%	18.2%
United States	45%	21.3%	33.7%
European Union	56.2%	19%	24.8%
China	17.4%	1.1%	81.5%
Japan	64.6%	9.9%	25.5%

Percentage of CO_2 coming from Oil, Natural Gas, and Coal.
http://infoweb.magi.com/~dwalsh/wfsesr.html

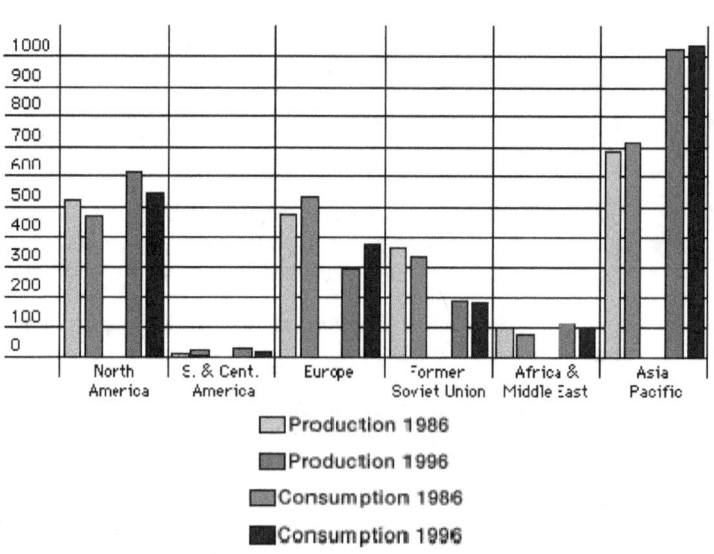

☐ Production 1986
☐ Production 1996
☐ Consumption 1986
■ Consumption 1996

How much coal different areas of the world have produced and consumed over time

Renewable Energy Sources

Hydro power, currently supplying only six percent of the world's energy, is a renewable energy source. Energy is produced by hydraulic turbines that rotate with the force of rushing water (higher to lower elevation).

It is one of the cleanest and cheapest ways of producing energy, but it can also change the flow of rivers and increase sediment which kills fish.

It is a large investment for developing countries.
ref: www.abcnews.com/sections/us/global106

Wind power emits no greenhouse gases, but it takes up large amounts of land. In order for it to be a reliable source, scientists must develop better power storage techniques.

Another concern of people is noise pollution that the large windmills produce along with the reliability of wind. **Solar power** uses photovoltaic cells (PV's) to gather thermal energy directly from the sun and use it to produce electricity. One community could be supplied by one field of PV's.

Passive solar cells could also be used to heat water, replacing the need for today's hot water heaters. PV's do not emit any greenhouse gases, but they are very expensive and more development is needed in order for this to be realistic energy source for the future.
ref: www.abcnews.com/sections/us/global106

 Nuclear power is strong is Europe with about forty-two percent of their energy produced by **fission.**

Nuclear generation provides about 17% of world electricity, avoiding the emission of up to 2.3 billion tonnes of carbon dioxide annually. France produces 76% and Lithuania produces 85.6% of its energy by nuclear fission.
ref: http://infoweb.magi.com/~dwalsh/wfsesr

In the United States, people are antinuclear because of 3 Mile Island in 1979 and Chernobyl in 1986. However, many experts say that it is a safe, clean, and reliable source of energy.

Nuclear Fission produces no greenhouse gases, but does produce highly toxic radioactive wastes.

Also available from the same author:

From a condensed history of the atom to its structure and then onto nuclear power, nuclear accidents and nuclear weapons. Intended for A-Level and High School studies, this book is ideally suited for almost all readers. Its 230 pages are supported by 180 diagrams, charts and pictures help towards making a complex subject into an 'easy read'.

> Available through all major book sellers including Amazon as a paper-back in black & white or Kindle in full colour.

www.ingramcontent.com/pod-product-compliance
Lightning Source LLC
Chambersburg PA
CBHW070340290526
45791CB00003B/1409